THE GREAT ZOO

PHOENIX POETS

Edited by Srikanth Reddy

Rosa Alcalá, Douglas Kearney &
Katie Peterson, consulting editors

The Great Zoo

A Bilingual Edition

NICOLÁS GUILLÉN
TRANSLATED BY AARON COLEMAN

THE UNIVERSITY OF CHICAGO PRESS
CHICAGO & LONDON

The University of Chicago Press, Chicago 60637
The University of Chicago Press, Ltd., London
El gran zoo ©2023 by Nicolás Guillén c/o Indent Literary Agency, LLC
Translation ©2024 by Aaron Coleman
For more information, contact the University of Chicago Press, 1427 E. 60th St., Chicago, IL 60637.
Published 2024
Printed in the United States of America

33 32 31 30 29 28 27 26 25 24   1 2 3 4 5

ISBN-13: 978-0-226-83479-5 (paper)
ISBN-13: 978-0-226-83480-1 (e-book)
DOI: https://doi.org/10.7208/chicago/9780226834801.001.0001

Library of Congress Cataloging-in-Publication Data

Names: Guillén, Nicolás, 1902–1989, author. | Coleman, Aaron, translator. | Guillen, Nicolas, 1902–1989. Gran zoo. Spanish. | Guillén, Nicolas, 1902–1989. Gran zoo English (Coleman)
Title: The great zoo : a bilingual edition / Nicolás Guillén ; translated by Aaron Coleman.
Other titles: Phoenix poets.
Description: Chicago ; London : The University of Chicago Press, 2024. | Series: Phoenix poets | Parallel text in Spanish and English.
Identifiers: LCCN 2024009748 | ISBN 9780226834795 (paperback) | ISBN 9780226834801 (ebook)
Subjects: LCGFT: Poetry.
Classification: LCC PQ7389.G84 G713 2024 | DDC 861.620877291—dc23/eng/20240305
LC record available at https://lccn.loc.gov/2024009748

♾ This paper meets the requirements of ANSI/NISO Z39.48-1992 (Permanence of Paper).

CONTENTS

INTRODUCTION

NICOLÁS GUILLÉN, MAKER AND BREAKER OF FORMS

Nicolás Cristóbal Guillén Batista was born at two in the morning on July 10, 1902, in the Camagüey province of east central Cuba. Both of his parents, Argelia Batista Arrieta and Nicolás Guillén Urra, were of African and European ancestry. At age fifteen Guillén—the oldest of six siblings—suffered the sudden loss of his father, a liberal political figure, who was assassinated by government forces for protesting electoral fraud. As a young adult, Guillén was immersed in the island's politics and burgeoning print culture. He worked at printing presses in his hometown of Camagüey and in Havana, where he moved to study law after graduating high school. The young writer eventually left behind his legal studies, finding his way instead into Havana's literary scene.

Guillén's best-known poems first appeared in 1930 in *Diario de la Marina*, one of the country's leading newspapers. Published as a suite titled *Motivos de son*—which I might translate as "motives of son" or "motifs of son"—they were both a roaring success and a scandal because they flouted the expectations of traditional poetry. Indeed, Guillén was a consummate maker and breaker of forms. The innovative poet rose swiftly to fame as he transformed the popular Cuban musical form of the *son* into a poetic form that called attention to the experiences of Afro-Cuban people and broke racial taboos.

Guillén continued to transform language and music throughout his career. At times he crafted poems born of Cuban slang and song, while in other moments, he satirized the supposed objectivity of journalistic and scientific writing. Through it all, Guillén traveled the island and the world, interweaving his artistic and political commitments to build a body of work admired by readers around the globe. Returning to the island in 1959 after spending much of the 1950s in exile, he was hailed as the national poet of revolutionary Cuba. Guillén's life spanned nine decades of the twentieth century before he passed away on July 16, 1989. His singular poetics evolved with his changing world—but his underexamined masterpiece *El gran zoo* (1967) defies expectations even today.

Swerving from the hilarious to the harrowing, *The Great Zoo* explores an uncanny menagerie of ideas and social concerns. Each poem is a cage in this literary exhibit, and the animals we encounter range from the Mississippi and Amazon Rivers, the North Star, clouds from different countries, and a hurricane to the KKK, the police, a guitar, and a dream. *The Great Zoo* also shines light on a turning point in Guillén's career—in these pages, the poet takes up another voice and form entirely. This new music moves in camouflage as it carries us through parodies of zoological language. I found myself equally stunned by Guillén's image-driven descriptions and how they upend a colonial history that has exoticized and demeaned living beings put on display for the sake of human whimsy. As a poet I've learned much from Guillén's forms: how the momentum of music can propel a collage of images and how images can resound with their own luminous music.

It's melting helplessly,
the North Star.
Ten million, or even more,
tons every day
(*ice, cold light, gas*)
waste away from the frame
of this immense animal.

These poems bear facets like diamonds: an image or phrase catches light and turns again and again in enjambed lineations, revolving from humor to sorrow to absurdity to wonder. I wonder what we might learn if we listen carefully to Guillén's imaginative but frighteningly real bestiary—to the roars and howls of its animals, to the clank and rattle of its cages, and to the underwater thump of the Caribbean within its aquarium. Guillén's humor shimmers here, in its darkness and in its lightness, as his poems wink at the world. These poems do indeed bite and dream, sing and "graze the cold hands of the moon."

Living between languages myself as a translator, a poet, and a child and student of the African diaspora, I'm astounded by how these poems open new vantage points and possibilities for contemporary audiences. To read Guillén across the diaspora, as he speaks out against colonialism and anti-Black violence, bears witness to Blackness beyond any single language, history, or country. To read his poems in translation in the United States today traverses political, geographic, linguistic, generational, and poetic boundaries.

I'm humbled and honored to follow in the footsteps of other Black poets translating between Cuba and the United States. This longer legacy includes the work of none other than that elder statesman of the Harlem Renaissance James Weldon Johnson, whose edited anthology *The Book of American Negro Poetry* (1922) included his own translation of the nineteenth-century Afro-Cuban poet Plácido (Gabriel de la Concepción Valdés), and Langston Hughes, who, along with the Howard University professor Ben Frederic Carruthers, produced the first English-language collection of Guillén's poetry, *Cuba Libre* (1948). Through the work of translation, we discover new ways of speaking our own languages: the imagination and craft of one writer finds new form in the imagination and craft of another.

This bilingual edition offers readers the opportunity to locate themselves in relation to Guillén's source poems and my translations. The far-reaching themes and emotional intensities of *The Great Zoo* open myriad pathways for visiting Guillén's carnivalesque vision. I have highlighted the legacy of what I call "Afrodiasporic translation" because I'm curious about translation's role in priming us to look backward and forward at the same time. I want to widen our gaze so that we see a diasporic constellation of translations—all while we dwell in the fantastical nature of Guillén's great zoo. The creative experiments of poets and translators, occurring between languages and locations, signal the vital potential of translation to shape the past, present, and future of the African diaspora.

Aaron Coleman
ANN ARBOR, MICHIGAN

THE GREAT ZOO

AVISO

Por un acuerdo del Ayuntamiento
fue creado este gran zoo
para nativos y extranjeros
y orgullo de nuestra nación.
Entre los ejemplares de más mérito
están los animales de agua y viento
(como en el caso del ciclón),
también un aconcagua verdadero,
una guitarra adolescente,
nubes vivas,
un mono catedrático y otro cotiledón.

¡Patria o muerte!

EL DIRECTOR

NOTICE

By resolution of the Local Authority
this great zoo was created
for natives and foreigners
and the pride of our nation.
Among the most prized specimens
are the water and wind animals
(as in the case of the hurricane),
also, a real live Aconcagua,
a teenage guitar,
living clouds,
one professor monkey, and another embryonic one.

Fatherland or Death!

THE DIRECTOR

EL CARIBE

En el acuario del Gran Zoo,
nada el Caribe.

       Este animal
marítimo y enigmático
tiene una cresta de cristal,
el lomo azul, la cola verde,
vientre de compacto coral,
grises aletas de ciclón.
En el acuario, esta inscripción:
                      "Cuidado: muerde".

THE CARIBBEAN

In the aquarium of the Great Zoo
the Caribbean slips by.

       This animal,
enigmatic and maritime,
has a crest of crystal glass,
a blue back, a green tail,
an underbelly of compact coral,
and the gray fins of a hurricane.
On the aquarium, this inscription:
                             "Caution: it bites."

GUITARRA

Fueron a cazar guitarras,
bajo la luna llena.
Y trajeron ésta,
pálida, fina, esbelta,
ojos de inagotable mulata,
cintura de abierta madera.
Es joven, apenas vuela.
Pero ya canta
cuando oye en otras jaulas
aletear sones y coplas.
Los sonesombres y las coplasolas.
Hay en su jaula esta inscripción:
                              "Cuidado: sueña".

GUITAR

They went out hunting for guitars,
underneath the full moon.
And they brought back her:
pale, fine, lithe,
ceaseless *mulata* eyes,
a waist of open wood.
She's young, just barely flies.
But already she sings
when she hears, in other cages,
the flittering wings of *sones* and *coplas*.
His somber*sones* and her lonely*coplas*.
On her cage is this inscription:

$$\text{"Caution: she dreams."}$$

ESCARABAJOS

Vean los escarabajos.
El de la India,
vientre de terracota y alas de fieltro azul.
Los Gemelos, de cobre y gutapercha.
El Imperial de Holanda
originario de Sumatra *(cobre solo)*.
El de lava volcánica
hallado en una tumba azteca.
El Gran Párpado de pórfido.

El de oro
(donación especial de Edgar Poe)
se nos murió.

BEETLES

See the beetles.
The one from India,
terra-cotta underbelly and blue-felt wings.
The Twins, copper and gutta-percha.
The Imperial from Holland,
originally from Sumatra *(only copper)*.
The one formed from volcanic lava,
found in an Aztec tomb.
The Great Eyelid of porphyry.

The gold one
(special donation from Edgar Poe)
died on us.

LA PAJARITA DE PAPEL

Sola, en su jaula mínima,
dormitando,
la Pajarita de Papel.

THE LITTLE PAPER BIRD

Alone, in her minimal cage,
dozing off,
the Little Paper Bird.

LA OSA MAYOR

Esta es la Osa Mayor.
Cazada en junio 4, 64,
por un sputnik cazador.
(No tocar las estrellas
de la piel).
    Se solicita
un domador.

THE URSA MAJOR

This is the Ursa Major.
Hunted down June 4, '64,
by a Sputnik on the prowl.
(Do not touch the stars
on its skin.)
                Now seeking
a tamer.

EL ACONCAGUA

El Aconcagua. Bestia
solemne y frígida. Cabeza
blanca y ojos de piedra fija.
Anda en lentos rebaños
con otros animales semejantes
por entre rocallosos desamparos.

En la noche,
roza con belfo blando
las manos frías de la luna.

THE ACONCAGUA

The Aconcagua. Beast,
solemn and frigid. Head,
white with eyes of motionless stone.
Travels in slow herds
with other similar animals
through rock-strewn desolations.

In the night,
its soft, heavy lips graze
the cold hands of the moon.

LOS USUREROS

Monstruos ornitomorfos,
en anchas jaulas negras,
los usureros.

Hay el Copete Blanco *(Gran Usurero Real)*
y el Usurero-Buitre, de las grandes llanuras,
y el Torpedo Vulgar, que devora a sus hijos,
y el Rabidaga de cola cenicienta,
que devora a sus padres,
y el Vampiro Mergánsar,
que chupa sangre y vuela sobre el mar.

En el ocio forzado
de sus enormes jaulas negras,
los usureros cuentan y recuentan sus plumas
y se las prestan a interés.

THE MONEYLENDERS

Ornithomorphic monsters
in lofty black cages,
the moneylenders.

There's the White Crested *(Great Royal Moneylender)*
and the Vulture-Moneylender, of the Great Plains,
and the Common Torpedo, which devours its children,
and the Daggerscut with its ashen tail feathers,
which devours its parents,
and the Vampire Cormorant,
which sucks blood and flies over the sea.

In the forced free time
of their vast black cages,
the moneylenders count and recount their feathers
and lend them to each other with interest.

LOS RÍOS

He aquí la jaula de las culebras.
Enroscados en sí mismos,
duermen los ríos, los sagrados ríos.
El Mississippi con sus negros,
el Amazonas con sus indios.
Son como los zunchos poderosos
de unos camiones gigantescos.

Riendo, los niños les arrojan
verdes islotes vivos,
selvas pintadas de papagayos,
canoas tripuladas
y otros ríos.

Los grandes ríos despiertan,
se desenroscan lentamente,
engullen todo, se hinchan, a poco más revientan,
y vuelven a quedar dormidos.

THE RIVERS

Here is the serpents' cage.
Coiled up on themselves,
the rivers, the sacred rivers, sleep.
The Mississippi with its Blacks,
the Amazon with its Indians.
They are like the powerful springs
of gigantic trailer trucks.

Laughing, children toss them
little green living islands,
parrot-painted jungles,
manned canoes,
and other rivers.

The great rivers wake up,
uncoil themselves slowly,
gobble down everything, swell, almost bursting,
and then go back to sleep.

SEÑORA

Esta señora inmensa
fue arponeada en la calle.

Sus pescadores arrojados
se prometían el aceite,
los bigotes delgados y flexibles,
la grasa . . . *(descuartizarla sabiamente)*.

Aquí está.

Convalece.

LADY

This immense lady
was harpooned in the street.

Her adventurous fishermen
were devoted to her oil,
her thin and flexible whiskers,
her blubber . . . *(carving it up skillfully)*.

Here she is.

Convalescing.

Al público

AVIO-MAMUT

*(Nota al pie de una foto al aire libre, de 3½ metros de
altura por 2 de ancho, que figura en el Gran Zoo).*

No era
la ruina de una avioneta,
como en un principio se creyó.
Era la osamenta
seca y abandonada de un mamut niño,
muerto en algún sitio de Siberia
y que un excursionista descubrió.

La avioneta es un ser mecánico,
y un gran sabio probó
que la osamenta tenía colmillos,
animal con más de un título
para estar en el Gran Zoo.

Pero como aquí
sólo se admiten ser vivos,
se ha dejado esta simple información,
con una foto de la pieza,
llamada *avio-mamut* de un modo ecléctico
para evitar cualquier otra discusión.

To the Public
AIR-MAMMOTH

*(Note at the foot of a photo, 3½ meters high
by 2 meters wide, on display in the open air of the Great Zoo.)*

It wasn't
the ruins of a small propeller plane,
as they had in the beginning believed.
It was the skeleton,
dry and abandoned, of a baby mammoth,
having died somewhere in Siberia
and been discovered by a backpacker.

The prop plane is a mechanical being,
and a great intellectual proved
that the skeleton had tusks,
an animal with more than enough credentials
to be in the Great Zoo.

But considering how here
only living beings are admitted,
they've set down this simple information
with a photo of the quarry,
called *air-mammoth* in an eclectic manner,
to avoid any other discussion.

LA SED

Esponja de agua dulce,
la sed.
Espera un río, lo devora.
Absorbe un aguacero.
Estrangula
con una cinta colorada.
¡Atención! ¡Las gargantas!

THE THIRST

Freshwater sponge,
the thirst.
It hopes for a river, devours it.
Absorbs a downpour.
Strangles
with a red-faced ribbon.
Warning! Throats!

EL HAMBRE

Ésta es el hambre. Un animal
todo colmillo y ojo.
Nadie lo engaña ni distrae.
No se harta en una mesa.
No se contenta
con un almuerzo o una cena.
Anuncia siempre sangre.
Ruge como león, aprieta como boa,
piensa como persona.

El ejemplar que aquí se ofrece
fue cazado en la India *(suburbios de Bombay)*,
pero existe en estado más o menos salvaje
en otras muchas partes.

No acercarse.

THE HUNGER

This is the hunger. An animal
all fang and eye.
No one cheats or distracts it.
It's not full after a meal.
It's not satisfied
by a lunch or a dinner.
It always announces blood.
Roars like a lion, squeezes like a boa,
thinks like a person.

The specimen offered here
was snared in India *(outskirts of Bombay)*
but exists in a more or less feral state
in many other places.

Don't come close.

INSTITUTRIZ

Catedrática.
Enseña inglés y álgebra.

Oxford.

Ramonea
hojillas tiernas, altas.
Casta, mas relativamente.

(Ama en silencio a un alumno elefante).

Nombre común: jirafa.

HEADMISTRESS

Professor.
Teaches English and algebra.

Oxford.

Grazes
on tender loose-leaves, high up.
Chaste, well, relatively.

(She loves, silently, a student-elephant.)

Common name: giraffe.

LAS NUBES

El Nubario.
Capacidad: 84 nubes.
Una experiencia nueva, porque hay
nubes de todo el día,
y de muchos países diferentes.
(*La Dirección anuncia más*).

Larguilenguas de pájaro,
rojizas,
las matutinas
hechas al poco sueño labrador
y a las albas vacías.
Detenidas,
de algodón seco y firme,
las matronales fijas del mediodía.
Como serpientes encendidas
las que anuncian a Véspero.
Curiosidad: Las hay de Uganda,
movidas por los vientos del gran lago Victoria.
Las del Turquino, bajas.
Las de los Alpes Marítimos.
Las del Pico Bolívar.
Negras, de gordas tetas,
las de tormenta.

También nubes románticas,
como por ejemplo las que empañan
el cielo del amor. Las coloreadas
de hace sesenta años
en los augurios de Noel.
Nubes con ángeles.
Nubes con formas de titán,
de mapas conocidos (*Inglaterra*),
de kanguro, león.
En fin, un cargamento respetable.

THE CLOUDS

The Cloud Sanctuary.
Capacity: 84 clouds.
A new experience, because there are
clouds from sunup to sundown
and from many different countries.
(*Management forecasts more.*)

Lanky-tongued like a bird,
reddish,
the daybreak clouds,
made by the farmer's brief dreams
and hollow dawns.
Restrained,
made of dry and firm cotton,
the motherly, immovable noonday ones.
Like serpents in flames,
the ones that announce the Evening Star.
A curiosity: there are some from Uganda,
driven by winds from the great Lake Victoria.
Some from El Turquino, lying low.
Some from the Maritime Alps.
Some from Pico Bolívar.
Black, with heavy breasts,
those of the storm.

Romantic clouds too,
like, for example, those that fog up
the sky of love. The rosy-colored ones
from sixty years ago
in the Christmas cards.
Clouds with angels.
Clouds the shapes of titans,
of well-known maps (*England*),
of kangaroos, lions.
In brief, a respectable load.

Sin embargo,
las de raza *Polar*, rarísimas,
no hubo manera de traerlas vivas.
Llegaron en salmuera, expresamente
de Groenlandia, Noruega, Terranova.
*(La Dirección ha prometido
exhibirlas al público en vitrinas).*

However,
these *Polar* breeds, extremely rare,
there was no way to bring them back alive.
They arrived in brine, express
from Greenland, Norway, Newfoundland.
(Management has promised
to exhibit them behind glass for the public.)

LOS VIENTOS

Usted no puede imaginar
cómo andaban estos vientos anoche.
Se les vio,
los ojos centelleantes,
largo y rígido el rabo.

Nada pudo desviarlos
(*ni oraciones ni votos*)
de una choza, de un barco solitario,
de una granja,
de todas esas cosas necesarias
que ellos destruyen sin saberlo.

Hasta que esta mañana los trajeron atados,
cogidos por sorpresa,
lentos enamorados,
cuando vagaban pensativos
junto a un campo de dalias.

(*Esos de allí, a la izquierda,*
dormidos en sus cajas).

THE WINDS

You cannot imagine
how these winds carried on last night.
They were seen,
eyes gleaming,
tailpieces stiff and long.

Nothing could knock them from their paths
(*not prayers, not promises*)
through a makeshift shack, a solitary boat,
and a plantation;
through all these necessary things
they so thoughtlessly destroy.

Until this morning, when they brought them back, tied up,
taken by surprise,
dawdling lovers,
as they wandered lost in thought
along a field of dahlias.

(*Those ones over there, to the left,*
sleeping in their boxes.)

EL TIGRE

Anda preso en su propia jaula
de duras rayas negras.
El metal con que ruge
quema, está al rojo blanco.
(Un gangster.
El instinto sexual.
Un boxeador.
Un furioso de celos.
Un general.
El puñal de amor).

Tranquilizarse.
Un tigre
real.

THE TIGER

It walks around captive in its own cage
of hard black stripes.
The metal within its roar
burns, is white-hot.
(A gangster.
The sexual instinct.
A boxer.
A jealous lover enraged.
A general.
The dagger of love.)

Please calm down.
This tiger
is real.

CICLÓN

Ciclón de raza,
recién llegado a Cuba de las islas Bahamas.
Se crió en Bermudas,
pero tiene parientes en Barbados.
Estuvo en Puerto Rico.
Arrancó de raíz el palo mayor de Jamaica.
Iba a violar a Guadalupe.
Logró violar a Martinica.
Edad: dos días.

HURRICANE

A thoroughbred hurricane,
just arrived in Cuba from the Bahamas.
Raised in Bermuda
but has family in Barbados.
Has been to Puerto Rico.
Ripped out the mainmast of Jamaica by the roots.
Was going to ravage Guadeloupe.
Did ravage Martinique.
Age: two days.

AVE-FÉNIX

Ésta es la jaula destinada
a la resurrección del Ave-Fénix.

(En diciembre llegarán sus cenizas).

PHOENIX

This is the cage destined
for the resurrection of the Phoenix.

(Its ashes will arrive in December.)

LYNCH

Lynch de Alabama.
Rabo en forma de látigo
y pezuñas terciarias.
Suele manifestarse
con una gran cruz en llamas.
Se alimenta de negros, sogas,
fuego, sangre, clavos,
alquitrán.

       Capturado
junto a una horca. Macho.
Castrado.

LYNCH

Lynch from Alabama.
Tailpiece in the form of a whip
and three-pointed hooves.
Tends to appear
with a great cross in flames.
Feeds on Black people, ropes,
fire, blood, nails,
tar.

        Captured
close to a hanging. Male.
Castrated.

EL CANGREJO

El terrible cangrejo que devora
senos, páncreas, próstatas,
hunde sus patas de insistencia fija
en un gran útero de plástico.
Destino limitado, pues no tiene
carne de estreno que morder,
linfa potable o sangre.

Tal vez no se ha querido
ofrecer todo el cuadro.
El Zoo, sin embargo,
brinda lo principal, ni más ni menos
que en otras importantes capitales.

A la derecha, junto al gangster.

THE CRAB

The terrible crab devours
breasts, pancreases, prostates;
sinks its fixed, insistent claws
into a great uterus made of plastic.
Its ends are limited, since it doesn't have
new meat to eat,
potable lymph, or blood.

Perhaps they do not want
to show the whole picture.
The Zoo, nevertheless,
imparts what is important; no more, no less
than other major capitals.

To the right, next to the gangster.

GANGSTER

Este pequeño gangster neoyorquino
es el hijo menor de un gangster de Chicago
y una madre *bull-dog*.
                    Fue herido en el asalto
al Royal Bank de Seattle.
Chester.
Lucky.
Camel.
White Label o Four Roses.
Browning.
Heroína.

(Sólo habla inglés).

GANGSTER

This little New York gangster
is the youngest son of a gangster from Chicago
and a mother-bulldog.
                              He was injured in the assault
on the Royal Bank of Seattle.
Chesterfield.
Lucky.
Camel.
White Label or Four Roses.
Browning.
Heroin.

(Only speaks English.)

KKK

Este cuadrúpedo procede
de Joplin, Misuri.
Carnicero.
Aúlla largamente en la noche
sin su dieta habitual de negro asado.

Acabará por sucumbir.
Un problema *(insoluble)* alimentarlo.

KKK

This quadruped comes
from Joplin, Missouri.
Meat eater.
On and on it howls through the night
without its regular diet of chargrilled Black folk.

In the end it will die.
Feeding it is a*(n unsolvable)* problem.

LAS ÁGUILAS

En esta parte están las águilas.
La caudal.
La imperial.
El águila en su nopal.
La bicéfala *(fenómeno)*
en una jaula personal.
Las condecoratrices
arrancadas del pecho de los condenados
en los fusilamientos.
La pecuniaria, doble, de oro $20 *(veinte dólares)*.
Las heráldicas.
La prusiana, de negro siempre como una viuda fiel.
La que voló sesenta años sobre el Maine, en La Habana.
La yanqui, traída de Viet Nam.
Las napoleónicas y las romanas.
La celestial,
en cuyo pecho resplandece Altaír.
En fin,
el águila
de la leche condensada marca "El Águila".
*(Un ejemplar
realmente original)*.

THE EAGLES

Here in this section are the eagles.
The golden, flowing one.
The imperial one.
The eagle atop its nopal.
The two-headed one *(a phenomenon)*
in a cage all its own.
The medal-decorated ones
ripped from the chests of the condemned
in front of firing squads.
The pecuniary one, doubled, $20 gold *(twenty dollars)*.
The heraldic ones.
The Prussian one, in all black, always, like a faithful widow.
The one that flew for sixty years over the *Maine*, in Havana.
The Yankee, taken back from Vietnam.
The Napoleonic ones and the Roman ones.
The heavenly one,
with the Altair star shimmering on its chest.
And finally,
the eagle
from that brand of condensed milk, Eagle.
(A model specimen,
truly original.)

MONOS

El territorio de los monos.
De acuerdo con los métodos modernos
están en libertad provisional.

El de sombrero profesor.
Con su botella el del anís.
Los generales con sus sables de cola.
En su caballo estatua el héroe mono.
El mono oficinista en bicicleta.
Mono banquero en automóvil.
Decorado mono mariscal.
El monocorde cordio
fásico cotiledón.
Monosacárido.
Monoclinal.
Y todos esos otros que usted ve.

Para agosto
nos llegarán seiscientos monosmonos.
(*La monería fundamental*).

MONKEYS

Monkey territory.
In accordance with modern methods,
they are on probation.

The one with the professorial hat.
With his bottle, the anisette one.
The generals with their saber tails.
Atop his horse statue, the hero monkey.
The office-worker monkey on a bicycle.
Banker monkey in an automobile.
Decorated field-marshal monkey.
The cardiac monochord monkey
at its placental start.
Monosaccharide monkey.
Monoclinal monkey.
And all the other ones you see.

For August
we'll receive six hundred primeprimates.
(*Fundamental monkey business.*)

PAPAYA

La papaya.
Animal
vegetal.
No es cierto
que conozca el pecado original.
Cuanto se diga,
mírenla,
es pura coincidencia. Sucia
literatura
que han padecido por igual
la calabaza y la sandía.
Cosas, en fin, de la abstinencia
(senil o juvenil)
sexual.

PAPAYA

The papaya.
Vegetal
animal.
It's not true
that it's familiar with original sin.
Whatever they may say—
look at it—
it's pure coincidence. Dirty
literature
under which gourds and watermelons
have suffered just the same.
Stuff, in the end, of abstinence
(senile or youthful),
sexual abstinence.

LUNA

Mamífero metálico. Nocturno.

Se le ve
el rostro comido por un acné.

Sputniks y sonetos.

MOON

Metal mammal. Nocturnal.

You can see
its face eaten by acne.

Sputniks and sonnets.

TENOR

Está el tenor en éxtasis
contemplando al tenor
del espejo, que es el mismo tenor
en éxtasis
que contempla al tenor.

Sale a veces a pasear por el mundo
llevado de un bramante de seda,
aplaudido en dólares,
tinta de imprenta
y otras sustancias gananciales.
(Aquí en el zoo le molesta
cantar por la comida
y no es muy generoso con sus arias).

Milán Scala.
New York Metropolitan.
Ópera de París.

TENOR

The tenor is in ecstasy
contemplating the tenor
in the mirror, which is the same tenor
in ecstasy
that contemplates the tenor.

Sometimes he steps out for a stroll around the world,
drawn along by a silken thread,
applauded in dollars,
printer's ink,
and other gainful substances.
(Here in the zoo he's bothered
to sing for food,
and he's not so generous with his arias.)

Milan's La Scala.
New York's Metropolitan.
Paris's Opera.

POLICÍA

Este animal se llama policía.
Plantígrado soplador.
Variedades: la inglesa, *sherlock. (Pipa).*
Carter, la norteamericana. *(Pipa).*
Alimento normal:
pasto confidencial,
electrointerrogograbadoras,
comunismo *(internacional)*,
noches agotadoras
de luz artificial.

Son mucho más pequeños los de raza *policeman.*
Metalbotones, chapa. La cabeza
formando gorra. Pelaje azul en general.
Alimento normal: delincuencia infantil,
disturbios, huelgas, raterías.
Comunismo *(local).*

POLICE

This animal calls itself police.
Whistling plantigrade.
Varieties: the English, *Sherlock*. *(Pipe.)*
Carter, the North American. *(Piece.)*
Typical diet:
confidential fodder,
electrointerrogataperecorders,
communism *(international)*,
grueling nights
of artificial light.

Quite littler are those of the race called *policeman*.
Metal buttons, badge. The head
formed into a cap. In general, a blue pelt.
Typical diet: juvenile delinquency,
disturbances, strikes, petty larceny.
Communism *(local)*.

EL CHULO

Orobotones en la camiseta
legítima H. R.
Rabocolt 38 con dril blanco espejo.
Cresta de Jipijapa.
Mimí Pinsón en el pañuelo.

Echado en el fondo de la jaula
pasa su poca vida y gran hastío
de sueño en sueño con las secas putas
(todas en estado cadavérico)
del viejo santo San Isidro.

Nota: ejemplar único, cazado
hace sesenta años
una noche de riña con franceses
en Luz y Curazao.

THE PIMP

Goldbuttons on his short-sleeve shirt,
authentic H&R
PrickColt .38 with hard white linen.
His crest a panama hat.
Mimi Pinson on his handkerchief.

Lying in the back of the cage,
he spends his little life and great boredom
in and out of dreams with the dry whores
(*all in a cadaverous state*)
of the old saintly San Isidro.

Note: a unique specimen, hunted down
sixty years ago
the night of a street fight with Frenchies
on the corner of Luz and Curazao.

RELOJ

Quiróptero
de una paciencia extraordinaria
no exenta de crueldad,
sobre todo
con los ajedrecistas y los novios.

Sin embargo,
es cordial a las 3 menos ¼
tanto como a las 9 y 15, los únicos momentos
en que estaría dispuesto a darnos un abrazo.

CLOCK

Chiroptera
of an extraordinary patience
not beyond cruelty,
above all
with chess players and lovers.

Still,
it's cordial at a quarter to three
and just the same at 9:15, the only times
when it's willing to give us a hug.

AVISO

GRAN ZOO DE LA HABANA

Museo de prehistoria abierto al público—todos los días
menos los domingos.—Idiomas: español, inglés y ruso.

Se avisa la llegada
de nuevos ejemplares, a saber:
La gran paloma fósil del jurásico
en la que son visibles todavía
sus dos dispositivos lanzabombas.
Hay una colección de hachas atómicas,
máscaras rituales de forma antiaerolítica
y macanas de sílex radioactivo.
Finalmente, un avión
(el tan buscado caza del plioceno)
que es una pieza de excepción.

La Habana, Junio 5.

EL DIRECTOR

NOTICE
GREAT ZOO OF HAVANA

The Museum of Prehistory now open to the public—every day
except Sundays.—Languages: Spanish, English, and Russian.

Now announcing the arrival
of new specimens, namely
the Great Pigeon-Dove fossil from the Jurassic,
in which are still visible
its two bayclaws for dropping bombs.
There's a collection of atomic axes,
ritual masks in the antimeteoric style,
and cudgels formed from radioactive flint.
Finally, an airplane
(the highly coveted predator of the Pliocene),
which is an exceptional piece.

Havana, June 5.

THE DIRECTOR

ORADORES

Aquí los oradores.
Algunos son campeones
provinciales. Otros
lo son olímpicos. Otros
no son nada, ni siquiera oradores.

Plumaje muy diverso.
Con todo, predomina
cierta *nuance* vulgar del amarillo.
Como usted nota,
la confusión es colosal.

> *Señoras y señores*
> *¡Camaradas!*
> *Amados hijos míos*
> *Señor presidente, señores diputados*
> *Respetable público*
> *¡Compañeros!*
> *Me siento emocionado*
> *Es ésta la primera vez*
> *Esta noche no debéis esperar de mí un discurso*
> *Permitidme que*
> *No sé cómo yo oso*
> *¡Qué distinta es, esclarecido Cristóbal Colón,*
> *Los familiares del difunto me*

Cuando al fin enronquecen hacen gárgaras
con las palabras que les sobran
(muy pocas)
y recomienzan la función:

> *y señores maradas*
> *esperar de mí un discurso*
> *jos míos respetable*
> *cionado*
> *funto cómo yo oso*
> *Colón*

ORATORS

Here, the orators.
Some are champions
of their hometowns. Others
are Olympians. Others
are nothing at all, not even orators.

Highly diverse plumage.
That being said, what predominates
is a certain vulgar *je ne sais quoi* in their yellow.
As you will observe,
the confusion is colossal.

>
> *Ladies and gentlemen*
> *Comrades!*
> *Beloved children of mine*
> *Mr. President, esteemed congresspersons*
> *Good and kind audience*
> *Friends!*
> *I am so excited*
> *This here is the first time*
> *Tonight, don't expect a speech from me*
> *Please allow me to*
> *Dare I say*
> *How distinctive he is, the renowned Christopher Columbus . . . !*
> *On behalf of the family of the deceased*

When they finally lose their voices, they gargle
with the words they have leftover
(*very few*)
and begin again the performance:

>
> *and gentlemen mrades*
> *expect a speech from me*
> *dren of mine good and kind*
> *xcited*
> *ceased dare I say*
> *Columbus*

EL SUEÑO

Esta mariposa nocturna
planea sobre nuestra cabeza
como el buitre sobre la carroña.
(El ejemplar
que aquí exhibimos es el sueño vulgar).

Sin embargo,
la dirección promete para fines de año,
o más pronto, tal vez,
remesas escogidas de sueños
así en hombre como en mujer.

Cinco cajas de moscas tse-tse
fueron pedidas anteayer.

THE DREAM

This nocturnal butterfly
glides over our heads
like a vulture over a carcass.
(Our model specimen
exhibited here is the everyday dream.)

Nevertheless,
management promises by year's end,
or even sooner, maybe,
choice parcels of dreams,
as many for men as for women.

Five boxes of tsetse flies
were ordered the day before yesterday.

GORILA

El gorila es un animal
a poco más enteramente humano.
No tiene patas sino casi pies,
no tiene garras sino casi manos.
Le estoy hablando a usted
del gorila del bosque africano.

El animal que está a la vista,
a poco más
es un gorila enteramente.
Patas en lugar de pies
y casi garras en lugar de manos.
Le estoy mostrando a usted
el gorila americano.

Lo adquirió
nuestro agente viajero en un cuartel
para el Gran Zoo.

GORILLA

The gorilla is an animal
all but entirely human.
It doesn't have paws but quasi feet;
it doesn't have claws but quasi hands.
I am talking to you
about the gorilla of the African forest.

The animal you see here
is all but
entirely gorilla.
Paws instead of feet
and quasi claws instead of hands.
I am showing you
the American gorilla.

It was acquired
by our emissary abroad at an outpost
for the Great Zoo.

TONTON MACOUTE

A René Depestre

Cánido
numeroso en Haití bajo la Era
Cuadrúpeda.
        Ejemplar
hallado en corral presidencial
junto a las ruinas
silvestres de palacio.
(Port-au-Prince).

Perdió la pata izquierda de un balazo
frente al Champ de Mars
en un tumulto popular.

Morirá en breves días
a causa de la herida de machete
que le hunde el frontal.

Se le está preparando una vitrina
en el museo de historia natural.

TONTON MACOUTE

For René Depestre

Canid,
abundant in Haiti during the Era
of the Quadruped.
                    Model specimen
found in the presidential corral
just next to the ruined
wilderness of the palace.
(Port-au-Prince.)

Lost its left paw to a bullet
in front of the Champ de Mars
in a popular uprising.

It will die in a few short days
due to the machete wound
sunken in its forehead.

They're now preparing its display case
in the Museum of Natural History.

BOMBA ATÓMICA

Ésta es la bomba. Mírenla.
Reposa dormitando. Por favor
no provocarla
con bastones, varillas, palos, pinchos,
piedras. Prohibido
arrojarle alimentos.
¡Cuidado con las manos,
los ojos!

       La Dirección
lo ha dicho y advertido,
pero nadie hace caso,
ni siquiera el Ministro.

Es un peligro bárbaro
este animal aquí.

ATOMIC BOMB

This is the bomb. Look at it.
Lying down, dozing. Please
don't bother it
with canes, sticks, stakes, skewers,
stones. It's prohibited
to feed it.
Careful with the hands—
the eyes!

          Management
has spoken and given warning,
but no one pays attention,
not even the State.

It's a barbaric danger,
this animal here.

LA ESTRELLA POLAR

Se descongela sin remedio
la Estrella Polar.
Diez millones, y aún más
diarios de toneladas
(hielo, luz fría, gas)
pierde de su estructura
este inmenso animal.

En los sitios vacíos
verán,
miren ustedes hacia allá,
cómo nuestro equipo restaurador
va colocando masas de algodón.
Pero eso no puede bastar
y dentro de cuatros siglos a lo sumo
los navegantes tendrán
que andar a tientas por el mar.

¡Qué responsabilidad!
El animal que más nos cuesta
y el que menos se puede conservar.

THE NORTH STAR

It's melting helplessly,
the North Star.
Ten million, or even more,
tons every day
(ice, cold light, gas)
waste away from the frame
of this immense animal.

You will see,
if you look just over there,
how our team of conservators
keeps putting puffs of cotton
in the empty spaces.
But this won't be enough,
and within four centuries at most,
navigators will have
to blindly feel their way across the sea.

What responsibility!
The animal that costs us most,
and the one we can conserve the least.

SALIDA

Aquí termina la visita de hoy.
Mañana será otro día
y volveremos al Gran Zoo.

Seguir la flecha
Al fondo (izquierda)
SALIDA
EXIT
SORTIE

EXIT

Here concludes our visit today.
Tomorrow's another day,
and we'll return to the Great Zoo.

Follow the arrow
all the way to the back (left)
EXIT
SALIDA
SORTIE

ACKNOWLEDGMENTS

Thank you to the editors at the Academy of American Poets, who first published versions of "THE ACONCAGUA," "THE CLOUDS," "KKK," "THE NORTH STAR," and "THE URSA MAJOR" at poets.org.

I will never forget the days I spent with the inimitable Nancy Morejón during her visit to Washington University in Saint Louis, Missouri. Connecting with her felt like an inflection point in the growth of this project. I extend my heartfelt gratitude to Profesora Morejón, who studied with Nicolás Guillén himself and is an internationally renowned poet, translator, and scholar in her own right. Her work and presence instilled in me a deeper sense of the intergenerational, international, and multilingual community of poetry that I still cherish today. I can't thank enough Elzbieta Sklodowska, Joseph "Pepe" Schraibman, and all those involved in bringing her and other Cuban writers to visit our campus and region.

I am grateful beyond words to the far-reaching creative community that supported me in the development of this project. Firstly, to Nicolás Hernández Guillén, Paula Canal, and the entire estate and team at the Fundación Nicolás Guillén: mil gracias, siempre. Secondly, to Srikanth Reddy, Rosa Alcalá, Douglas Kearney, Katie Peterson, David Olsen, Lily Sadowsky, Adrienne Meyers, and Alan Thomas of the University of Chicago Press's Phoenix Poets series for seeing the potential of this work and for their vital guidance throughout the editorial process. Thirdly, to the following writers, translators, educators, and thinkers, whose expertise and inspirational kindness were essential in bringing this project to life: Hanif Abdurraqib, Esther Allen, Noh Anothai, Ali Araghi, Baba Badji, Mary Jo Bang, Espelencia Baptiste, Curtis Bauer, Layla Benitez-James, Devyn Spence Benson, Susan Bernofsky (a thousand thanks!), Sam Bett, Daniel Borzutzky, Geoffrey Brock, Catherine Brown, J. Dillon Brown, Jericho Brown, Bonnie Chau, Jon Cho-Polizzi, Kaché Claytor, Kristiana Rae Colón, Matthew Countryman, Kwame Dawes, Mónica de la Torre,

Elena del Pozo, Katrina Dodson, Sharon Dodua Otoo, Kristin Dykstra (thank you for your early guidance!), Frieda Ekotto, Marguerite Feitlowitz, Yomaira Figueroa Vásquez, Carmen García Méndez, Kaiama Glover, Matthias Göritz, Rav Grewal-Kök, Katherine Hedeen, Michael Holtmann, Ignacio Infante (my intrepid dissertation advisor!), A. Van Jordan, John Keene, Ryan James Kernan, Aliyah Khan, the late Mazisi Kunene and his family, Lawrence La Fountain-Stokes, Olivia Lott, Bertin Louis, Ali Maki, Roberto Márquez, Felipe Martínez, Miriam Martínez Taboada, Philip Matthews, William J. Maxwell, Christi Merrill, Charleen McClure, Peggy McCracken, Seipati Mokhosi, John Murillo, Urayoán Noel, Arantxa Oteo, Olasope Oyelaran, Leonardo Padura, Benjamin Paloff, Gregory Pardlo, Orlando Luis Pardo Lazo, Anca Parvulescu, Tiffany Ruby Patterson, Katja Perat, Carl Phillips, Todd Portnowitz, Yopie Prins, Sughey Ramírez, Renée Ragin Randall, Giulia Riccò, Aaron Robertson, Roque Raquel Salas Rivera, Niloofar Sarlati, Diane Seuss, Anton Shammas, Siyabonga Lebohang Sikhakhane, Timea Sipos, William Stroebel, Corine Tachtiris, Lynne Tatlock, Kira Thurman, Lance Tooks, Antoine Traisnel, Kārlis Vērdiņš, Phillip B. Williams, Eileen Wilson-Oyelaran, Leslie Wingard, Amy Wright, Matvei Yankelevich, Rafia Zafar, Janine Zagel, Pablo Zavala, and our entire Poetry Slam Madrid crew from Café Libertad. I also want to shout out the creative writing, comparative literature, English, Black studies, Romance languages, and library communities of the University of Michigan and Washington University in Saint Louis for indispensable support.

I will always be grateful for the thoughtful panel discussion John Keene, Kristin Dykstra, Tiffany Higgins, Lawrence Schimel, and I had at the Association of Writers & Writing Programs Conference, exploring the concerns raised by Keene in his landmark Poetry Foundation essay "Translating Poetry, Translating Blackness." I am also grateful for my collaborations with organizations such as the American Literary Translators Association, the Association for the Study of the Worldwide African Diaspora, Bennington College, Cave Canem, the Center for the Art of Translation, the City University of New York, Kalamazoo College, the Modern Language Association, and Saint Louis University, which offered me opportunities to think out loud about the stakes of translating Guillén and exploring Afrodiasporic translation today.

A special thank you to my brilliant, compassionate partner, Andrea Bolivar, for more than I can ever say. I also want to thank my parents and all my family (blood and chosen) for their patience and loving support as this project took shape over so many years. GBC, we all we got! Y finalmente, una y otra vez, gracias de todo corazón al poeta increíble Nicolás Guillén. Qué honor y regalo conocer tu poesía.